ZC HORSES

Sonny The Spectacular

Diane W. Keaster

illustrated by Toni Becker

ISBN 978-0-9721496-9-3

Printed in Montana

ZC HORSES

Sonny The Spectacular

To Chick.

April 25, 1975-September 20, 2006

ZC HORSES
SERIES

Be part of them all!

Chick - The Beginning!

Chick - The Saddle Horse!

Chick - The Mom!

Luke - The First!

Barbie - The Best!

Leroy - The Stallion!

And Many More!

ZC HORSES

Sonny The Spectacular

TABLE OF CONTENTS

1

The Women

Many times, when a person thinks of a rancher, they think of a man. Many times, though, the ranching involves a woman. This has been the case in my life.

My father had been involved in ranching from the time he was born. So was my mother. Her Grandpa Rush traveled from Ireland to Montana to become a rancher. Her father, at one time, was involved in ranching with Grandpa Rush. This was my Grandpa Fluhr.

Grandpa Rush leased a summer pasture near the Canadian border. This pasture was along the Milk River. The closest town was Browning, Montana.

To lease pasture means you do not own the ground. You pay an amount to let your cows or horses eat the grass on the land. This area had very tall, thick grass for the cows to eat.

One time my grandfather and my mother's grandfather were watching over the cows at this pasture.

My mother was a very little girl. Her mother took her to see the cows and the men. This was in the early 1930s. The cows were very far from any house or town. There had been much rain before my mother and grandmother took this trek. When they were almost in the middle of nowhere, their car stopped. That car would be well over 70 years old today. It was stuck in the slippery, thick mud. They could not move forward or backward. Since not many people visit the middle of nowhere, there was no help. They had to sleep in the car. They snuggled together with a warm blanket over them.

There were no sounds of cars or trucks through the night. The only sound was the continuous howling of sneaky coyotes. The dark, starry sky covered them. The stars winked at them continually through the night's dark sky.

After the sun rose into the blue sky, a cowboy on his horse spied the stranded car. He rode for help. They were finally rescued.

Later in the summer the cows were moved to a pasture set against Glacier National Park. The park's majestic mountains rose near in the background. They wore their white glacier caps. My mother and her parents slept in a tent at this pasture. One time they heard more than a coyote's howl. They also heard a bear's claws scraping down the side of the canvas tent. He wanted to stay with them, too! My grandfather made noise by hitting a pan. "CLANG, CLANG, CLANG!!" Afraid of the noise, the bear decided to stay someplace else.

When my mother was young, her love for horses was very strong. She rode her horse across the same ground her grandfather did. Her grandchildren ride their horses across that same ground today.

Because of my mother's interest in horses, I am here today. You see, before they were married, my father was training some of her mother's horses. My father was given one of the horses for training the rest. He always joked he liked my mother's horse better so he had to marry her to get it. I know there was a little more to it than that!

Because of both my parent's love for horses, I acquired that love. My love was very deep for one beautiful horse I had!

2

The New Father

Chick, my beautiful palomino (golden colored) mare was a horse I truly loved. I thought of her as my best friend. My dog Pete was my best friend, too! He was black and brown with a pointed nose.

When a female horse is too young to have babies, it is called a filly. When it is old enough to have babies, it is called a mare.

Chick had already given me four

wonderful babies. I loved them all. I already broke them. To break a horse means you train it to ride. I was riding Luke, Barbie, Goldie, and Chickadee. I enjoyed riding them as much as I did Chick.

It was exciting having a new baby. The most exciting thing was getting to see what color it would be. Two of Chick's babies turned out to be palomino, like her. They were Luke and Goldie. The other two, Barbie and Chickadee, wore their father's gray coat.

I decided this year to have a sorrel stallion be the father of Chick's baby. A sorrel is a red colored horse. Its mane and tail are usually the same color as its coat. He was a beautiful stallion that was ridden and used in the mountains.

To make sure I wanted him to be the father, I went to see him. He was standing out in a field grazing, or eating grass. This field was along the same river where I lived. It was the Sun River. It was very wide and flowed into the Missouri. I could imagine him running across a field. I could also imagine his baby running behind him, whinnying. The baby could possibly look just like him. That was it. He was the one for sure.

It was exciting to have this baby's father be sorrel. Luke's father was chestnut. A chestnut's body is dark red or reddish brown. They are a little darker than a sorrel. Its mane and tail sometimes may be a little darker than its body. A chestnut horse sometimes wears a flaxen mane and tail. That means there are light streaks through it. A hair stylist is not even needed to get the streaks! The father of the other three was gray. Sometimes babies turn out to be like their father. Sometimes they look like their mother. I had a little over eleven months to see if this foal would be the color of Chick or the color of its father.

Another thing to wonder was whether the foal would be a colt (a boy) or a filly. Chick had already had three fillies and one colt.

Maybe this time I would get a colt!

Once again, how could I wait!

3

The New Baby

As always, the wait to see what the baby was going to be took forever. During this time, Chick was pastured in a nice, green pasture. Rising high above were tall waving trees to shelter her. Off to the side of her was the muddy Sun River.

Chick was a very large mare. When she was not going to have a baby, she weighed 1450 pounds. Horses of the quarter horse breed, like she was, are usually very stocky. This is a very heavy weight for them. A nice sized horse is around 1200 pounds.

When Chick was going to have a baby, she was very heavy. In fact, when a mare or cow is carrying a baby, that is what they are called. If one is called ‘heavy’, it is carrying a baby.

Chick’s being so large did not stop her from running and bucking across the pasture. As big as she was, she was very agile. Her father had been a race horse. His father was, too. This is why Chick ran very fast. Once she was running at her fastest speed. She did not stop soon enough at a fence. I watched in horror. Without even thinking, Chick jumped the brown, wooden fence. The fence was almost five feet tall. There was even space between her and the fence! She was quite proud of herself for doing this! I was proud of her, too! Watching this did make me think twice about running her toward a fence while I was riding her, though.

As I always did, I watched Chick continually when the time was near for her to foal. Although the time varies, the time a mare carries her baby is eleven months and eleven days. This time will be longer as the mare gets older. The time also gets longer if the mare has had several foals.

Chick was close to the house. I thought maybe this time I would get to see her foal drop (or be born). Mares do not like to be watched when they are foaling. They are very sneaky about it, too! Chick was the sneakiest, I think!

Most of Chick's other foals were born on April 25 or close to it. Chick was born on April 25. This date was too early for this foal to drop. I did not get nervous until May. All of the wild flowers were blooming now. Chick's field was dotted with yellow, blue, pink, and orange. It seemed each flower sent its own smell at different times.

When Chick's date to foal had

come, I watched even more closely. Once again, Chick did not allow me to see this foal being born. It was in the middle of a beautiful spring day when I saw her. Chick's pure white mane was flowing in the slight breeze. The wind was singing its song through the leaves of the trees. There nursing on Chick, or drinking milk from her, was her precious new baby. I did not even need to get close to see its color. It was the spittin' image of her mom. (In Montana that's how we say they were identical.) This baby was a beautiful palomino with a pure white mane and tail. Now to find out if it was a colt or filly.

Chick never minded my going up

to her when her babies were born. Junie did. She chased my son Gus. She tried to stomp him to keep him away from her baby! Chick gave me a little nicker (or soft whinny) when I got to her. I could see right away this beautiful foal was a filly. I held her in my arms like I had held all the other foals. She was so sweet, unlike Chickadee and Barbie!

This filly shone as bright as the sun. This is the reason I dubbed her Sonny.

Although they had the same mother, Sonny was much different from her siblings!

4

The Princess

Chick's first four foals all had the same conformation (or build) and head shape. Just like with people, a horse usually is built the same way as its parents. They will also have the same shape of head. Chick, her children, and their fathers were quarter horses. One characteristic of this breed of horse is a very muscular rear end.

Chick and her children so far all were built that way.

I was surprised that Sonny did not look like her brother and sisters. She was not even close to having the heavy, stalky build of her mother. She had the most beautifully shaped head and body. The way she moved was eloquent. In fact, she looked like a beautiful princess. She moved with grace and style. I could not believe a horse's mane and tail could be so pure white. It flowed with every movement.

Sonny was a lighter palomino. She was more like her sister Goldie. Her white blaze still glistened like a neon light. A blaze is a wide strip of white down a horse's head. It goes at least from between the horse's eyes down to between its nostrils. If it is only in the center part of the horse's head, it is called a strip. If it is wider, it is said the horse is bald face.

Sonny's speech was even different. She did not have a low harsh whinny. Nor did she have a high squealing whinny. Her nicker was so soft I could hardly hear it.

Whatever Sonny did, she looked classy. Her walk was stylish. It was as if she was sailing across a smooth lake when she loped. Her silky mane and tail waved like a flag in the wind. If I had not seen the blanket of green under her feet,

I would have thought she was floating through the air.

Sonny's spectacular looks and conformation remained the same. No matter what age she was, she was gorgeous.

Beneath Sonny's sweet looks was a surprise waiting for me, though!

5

The Schooling

I trained Sonny just as I did all of my foals. When she was just born, I started training her. I wrapped my arms around her soft, furry body. While hugging her, I stroked her ears, back, and legs. I whispered softly into her ears, "Everything will be alright." At first she was scared. Her brown eyes opened so wide I saw the white around them. Her fuzzy ears stood straight up. This meant she was paying attention to me.

A horse has a very distinct smell. It is not offensive or disgusting. It is a smell all its own. With my face close to Sonny's, her scent surrounded me. Since she was just a little baby, her smell was very pleasing and pure. Everything about Sonny seemed sweet as candy!

Sonny's body felt tense in my arms. She was nervous for awhile. I kept stroking her for a bit. Then I felt one muscle relax. As I embraced her I felt another muscle relax. Her little body finally loosened up. She let out a deep breath with a "Swoosh". The whites in her eyes disappeared. Her eyes held a kind look now. Holding her when she was just born helped her trust people. I held her like that every day for several days.

When Sonny was three days old, I put a little blue halter on her head. The halter goes around the horse's nose, over its head, and behind its ears. This is the same halter Sonny's sisters and brother wore when they were just three days old. This halter was much smaller than Chick's! It had to be tiny to fit the baby's head.

I then fastened a rope onto the halter under Sonny's chin. This is called a lead rope. This is how you lead a horse. If a horse has never worn a halter before, they are not used to being held back. They may fight and pull away from you. Once the horse gets used to the halter and lead rope, they usually will not pull back. Sonny did not fight me like Barbie and Chickadee. She followed right behind me when I taught her to lead. The reason I broke my horses to lead when they were so young was because they were small. I was not strong enough to hold back an older, more powerful horse.

When Sonny was a year old she had been weaned for several months. Weaning her means I separated her from Chick. She then had to learn to eat on her own rather than nursing on Chick. While I had broke Sonny to lead, I had not snubbed her up to a post. She needed to learn to be tied up. Quite often, the horse will fight terribly when they are first tied up. Sonny had to get used to this, though, as she would be tied up many times in her life. It is bad if a horse ever pulls back while it is tied and breaks the lead rope. It thinks, then, if it pulls back it can get loose. It may always pull back when it is tied or pressure is put on the lead rope. This is a very bad habit for a horse to have. Chick's great-granddaughter Classy is like that sometimes.

When I first tied Sonny up, she was fine. She did not pull back or fight. While she was tied, I rubbed all over her soft body with a blanket. This is called sacking a horse out. Doing this would make it easier to put the saddle on the first time. That way, too, Sonny would not spook, or get scared, if something touched her.

I knew I had to wait until Sonny was two to start riding her. I did not want to push her before that. A horse can get too confused if you ride it younger than that. If that happens, they never make a good riding horse. It is said they have become 'soured'. Even when you start a horse at two, you must ride them easy. I did, though, saddle Sonny up as though I was going to ride her. This was well before she turned two. She did not mind the saddle and blanket at all.

This is why I was shocked at what happened!

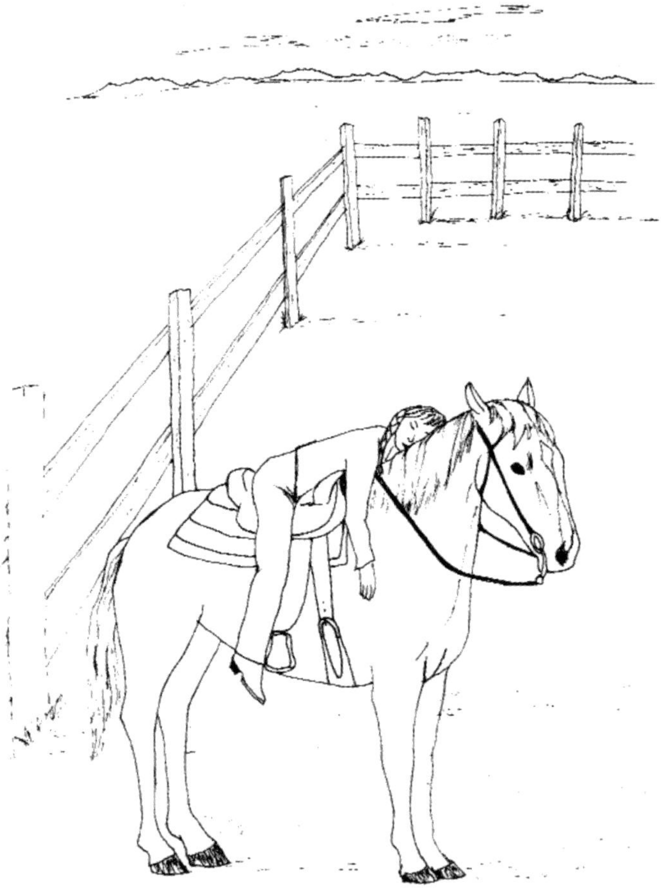

6

The First Ride

When Sonny was two years old, it was time to ride her. I just knew she would be fine. She had been wonderful about all of her training up to this point.

After I had saddled Sonny, I led her to a little pen. It is good if the size of the pen where you first get on a horse is small. If the horse wants to buck, it can not buck as hard if it has to go around the pen. The farther straight the horse can go the harder it will buck.

I first led Sonny around the pen a few times. After you saddle a horse, you should lead them a few steps. This will help to see if they might buck. It gets them used to the cinch being tight around their belly, too. My first time on any horse I always thought about Chick. She seemed so sweet until the second day I rode her. I was on the ground quicker than I was on her!

I had a ring snaffle bit in Sonny's mouth. There was a large ring on each side of her mouth. There was a bar that bent in the middle that crossed over her tongue. The bar hooked onto each ring. The bit is to control the horse. The first few times you ride it, though, there is no control. I always wore my chinks and cowboy hat. I figured if I did get bucked off, they would give me some protection. Chinks are shorter than chaps. They come right below your knee. They are leather and wrap around your legs. Mine were pink and gray. They were very smooth from wearing them so much while riding.

I stood on the left side of Sonny. She was looking back at me. It was the same as she did when I held her the day she was born. With my left hand, I grabbed the side of her bridle so she could not take her head and run. I had the reins in that hand, too. The reins are the leather straps attached to the bit so you can control the horse. I gently put my left foot into the stirrup on the saddle. I watched Sonny's eye the whole time. At first I put a little of my weight onto the stirrup. She did not seem to mind that.

Once I felt I was ready, I started to ease up into the saddle. Once you start going, you have to get your right leg over the horse's back. This needs to be done quickly but softly. I did this with Sonny. I started raising into the air. Then...........then........then....... I don't know what happened.

The next thing I knew, I woke up on Sonny's back. I was sitting in the saddle. We were walking slowly around the pen. I could not even remember getting on her. I always checked my watch and kept track of how long I rode. Quite a bit of time had passed.

A boy was watching me ride. I got off and went over to him. He saw what happened. He said right when I got on Sonny, she blew up bucking. She was bucking very hard. I got bucked off. I then lay on the ground for quite awhile. Sonny quit bucking when I went off. That was nice of her I thought. I thought it would have been even nicer for her to stop while I was on her. She was concerned about me, I guess! The boy said I got up, then, and got right on her. We had been going around the pen that whole time with me not knowing!

Fortunately, Sonny and I never had that problem again.

Really, though, I guess it was in the family!

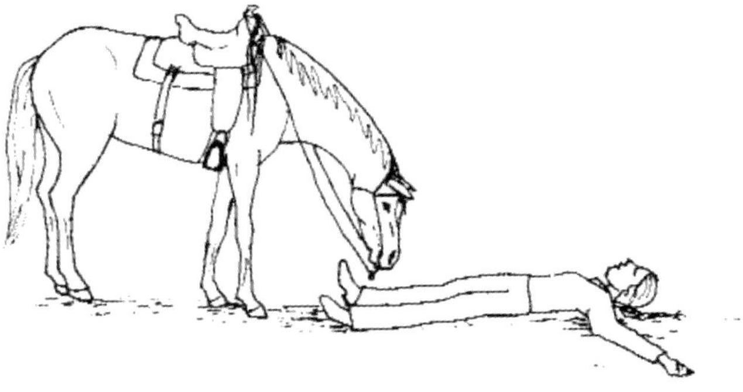

7

The Buck

Just like in certain families, horse families have certain traits. Bucking must have been something Chick's family liked to do once in awhile. Chick and her offspring bucked a little only at certain times. They certainly would not have been good as the bucking horses at rodeos. My sons Cole and Gus ride them.

Once when Barbie, Sonny's sister,

was four I had her saddled up and tied to the hitching post. The hitching post was next to the weathered red barn. A hitching post is a rail between two posts set solid in the ground. This makes a secure place to tie a horse in case they pull back.

I untied Barbie and went to lead her around to make sure she would not buck with me. We were heading to the arena to practice roping. The stirrup on the saddle hooked on the end of the hitching post. This spooked her. She pulled the lead rope out of my hand and blew up bucking. She bucked around in circles. She would not stop. A big dust cloud formed from her bucking so hard. A low grunt slipped from her throat each time she went into the air.

The horse trailer was sitting near-by. The door was open. I had been unloading hay from it. Without stopping bucking for a second, Barbie hopped into the trailer. "KERPLUNK" her feet echoed on the wooden floor. She was safe at last from that scary hitching post! When her feet landed, she stopped bucking and stood. Her neck was lathered up from sweat. She did not have a nice horse smell!

Barbie's son Leroy must have learned that trick from her. I had just caught him in a big field. We were going riding to a mountain lake on the top of the snow-capped mountain nearby. The air was brisk that day. I threw the saddle on and led him to the trailer. Right when we got to the trailer, something spooked him. Like mother like son, he blew up bucking. He was bucking so hard I could not keep hold of the lead rope. He went bucking down the road as fast as he could. It sounded like a tambourine clashing every time his feet hit the hard road.

I finally caught up with Leroy and he was fine. We went for a nice ride to the lake.

Even though Sonny bucked like her sister and nephew, things did change!

8

The Riding

One place to train a horse is in a round pen. It is a small corral in the shape of a circle. A round pen is a good place to train a horse. The horse can not sneak into a corner and stand there. It is always moving around. The training can be done with you on the horse's back. It can also be done with you standing in the middle of the pen with a small whip. This way you can holler out commands to the horse. The horse will learn to listen to you. You can tell the horse to stop, trot, lope, turn, or do whatever you want.

Riding Sonny along a fence helped her to learn to turn when I asked her to. At first I had to pull her head around in the direction I wanted. When I pulled the rein on the left side of Sonny, the rein on the right side touched her neck. When I pulled the rein on the right side to make her go right, the rein on the left side touched her neck there. Sonny learned when the rein touched her neck, she was to turn in the opposite direction. She also learned if she went in that direction right away, the bit would not touch her mouth, making things easier on her. Turning Sonny into the fence made her learn to neck rein faster.

I rode Sonny in a smaller pen at first. Then I started riding her outside. This way she got used to riding across creeks (pronounced to rhyme with 'sticks' in Montana). She also got used to me getting on and off her to open gates. She learned not to spook when pheasants shot up like missiles into the air right in front of her. She did not even mind the ominous rattle of the rattle snake. One thing she questioned was an antelope buck (a male). It is a deer-like animal with two long slender horns on its head. The buck tossed a frightful glare at us. With a short “HSSS” “HSSS” like a snake he warned us. That was his way of saying he did not want us there.

Riding Sonny in the Spring was so special. The air smelled fresh with the new flowers squeezing their heads out of the ground. Many times the only sound to be heard was the muffled stomp of her hooves on the frozen ground. Sonny always rode so nicely. She did everything right. She was as beautiful with her saddle on as she was without it!

Training Sonny was especially rewarding getting her ready for her special event!

9

The Sale

I owned many other horses when Sonny came along. Even more than Chick and her children. I knew I could not give attention to all of them. I had to make a tough decision. I decided my goal with Sonny was to break her and then sell her. This was sad for me. It was also exciting. If the people that raised Chick had not decided to sell her at a sale, I never would have known her. It made me sad to think of all the happiness I would not have known if I had not met Chick.

Quite often there are horse sales once a month. These are at a regular auction barn. An auction is

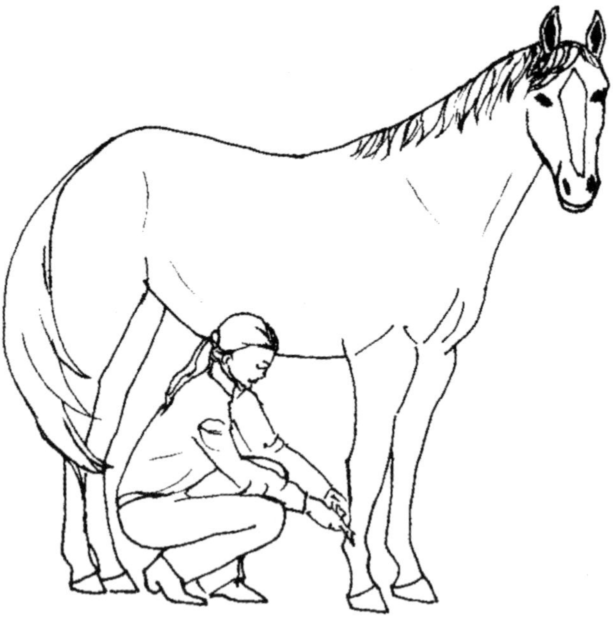

where animals are sold. A person can load up a horse and take it right into these sales.

Then there are fancy horse sales. Quite often they are called catalogue sales. That is because a write up about each horse is in a catalogue. These only happen every so often. Most of the time your horse has to get approval to be in these sales. There are certain medical tests that have to be done on the horse. These are to make sure they do not have any infection that could be spread to other horses. The horse has to be quite spectacular to be in the sale. Sonny fit the bill there!

I decided which special sale to sell

Sonny. It was during the Montana State Winter Fair. This was held in Bozeman, Montana. It was odd selling Sonny there because that is where I had Chick for awhile. I was taking her to school there with me when she saved me from freezing to death.

To put Sonny into this sale, I had to enter her months before it. Once she was accepted, I had a lot of work to do.

Along with training Sonny, I had to make sure she looked her best. I thought, "How could she look any better!" There is hair that grows long on a horse's fetlock. That is the part of the leg on the back just above the horse's ankle. This all has to be cut or shaved off. I had to also cut the long hairs off of Sonny's face and under her chin. I cut a nice smooth area in Sonny's mane right behind her ears at the top of her neck. I should have cut the hair out of her ears. I left it since it was Winter. I did not want her ears to get cold. Removing the long hairs on her legs, head, and mane made Sonny look very polished. She did not enjoy hearing the "BUZZZZ" of the electric clippers around her. Especially near her ears!

Since I was riding Sonny every day, I had shoes on her feet. This way she would not get tender from stepping on rocks. A horse needs to have their hooves, or feet, trimmed about every six weeks. Their hard feet grow quickly, just like our fingernails. If the shoes are not too worn, they are put back on. In this instance it is said the horse is reset. If the shoes are getting worn, the horse gets new ones. Once a horse has shoes on, it is said they are 'shod' (rhymes with trod). Damage can be done to a horse's leg or foot if the shoes are left on too long. They can not walk correctly with long hooves.

It was finally sale day. Sonny looked very good. I had given her a bath using special shampoo to make her furry coat look clean and shiny. Her coat was not slick as the sale was in the middle of winter. The summer heat and long days makes a horse lose their shaggy hair. If you leave a horse in a barn with the light on all of the time, their hair will start coming off. Her silky white mane and tail glistened in the sun. I ran a comb through it with ease. I sprayed a special hair conditioner on it to make it shine even more.

Sonny's hooves looked good since I just had her shod. I painted them with a black, shiny polish to make them look even better. She looked so nice with all the straggly hairs trimmed off.

When I bought Chick at the horse sale, she was too young to be ridden. That is why she was led in. Since Sonny was now broke, I rode her into the sale ring. I made sure I used my fanciest headstall and saddle to dress her up. The headstall is a leather piece. It goes behind the ears and down the side of the horse's head. It holds the bit in place. Just like with Chick, everyone was in awe over how beautiful she was. She was not nervous at all. She ignored all the talking and commotion around her. She walked her princess-like strut as if she was a model.

Many people bid on Sonny, or tried to buy her. One special young girl ended up being the last person to bid. She got to buy Sonny. I was amazed when I met her. Her name was also Sonny! I could tell she immediately loved Sonny as much as I loved Chick when I bought her. Sonny's new home was going to be Drummond, Montana, where I saw her often.

All of my hard work with Sonny paid off. I had the top-selling mare at the sale. This was a special privilege, meaning my mare sold for more money than anyone else's.

Although I did not own Sonny anymore, she was always with me!

10

The Memory

I once heard that memories are like starlight and starlight goes on forever. That is how memories are of ones we love. We have so many special memories, they seem to go on forever. It does not matter if we go away for a long time. It does not matter that we are just apart for a little while. If we hold onto those memories and special moments, that individual will always be with us. Our hearts can never be too full of ones we love! Once we have felt that love, those memories will stay with us forever.

To have memories of ones we love, we need to spend time together. The more time we spend, the more memories we will have. The times I had with Sonny were very precious to me. She was a spectacular horse. I have many special memories of her. Looking at Chick, I always thought of Sonny.

Even though Sonny is not with me physically, she will always be in my heart.

ZC HORSES SERIES

Now that you have gotten to know Chick and some of her children and one of her grandchildren, get ready to meet a different breed of horse that joined in with them! You will have the opportunity to learn about Idaho's State Horse, the Appaloosa. Chick got to know a few of this breed now you can, too, in the eleventh in the **'ZC HORSES'** series, ***"Appaloosa-The State Horse"***.

Be sure to be there to greet them!!

ZC HORSES SERIES #11

Appaloosa-The State Horse

by Diane W. Keaster

Coming Winter 2007

To My Reader:

I was born and raised on a ranch near a little town called Belt, Montana. After receiving my B.S. in Business Education from Montana State University, I taught high school business. I then moved on to other facets of employment.

The whole time, I was team roping and raising, breaking, and training horses. The profession I fell into by mistake was trading horses. Throughout my life I have handled hundreds of horses, all which have a story of their own.

My sons, Cole and Augustus, loved reading stories about horses when they were small and I loved reading the stories to them. That is why I am writing these books. I want to tell the stories of the creatures I love to the children I love.

I thank Jehovah our Creator for giving us such a wonderful, beautiful animal!

Enjoy the stories!

Order Form

ZC HORSES SERIES

Don't miss out on any part of the lives of Chick and her many babies and friends! Experience all of the rides, joys and sorrows. Don't be left out!

___	Chick-The Beginning! (Spring 2001)	$6.95
___	Chick-The Saddle Horse! (Summer 2001)	$6.95
___	Chick-The Mom! (March 2002)	$6.95
___	Luke-The First! (July 2002)	$6.95
___	Barbie-The Best! (Oct. 2002)	$6.95
___	Leroy-The Prize (Summer 2003)	$6.95
___	Goldie-The Wise (February 2004)	$6.95
___	Chickadee-The Traveler (September 2004)	$6.95
___	Darby-The Cow Dog (October 2005)	$6.95
___	Sonny-The Spectacular (Nov. 2006)	$6.95
___	Appaloosa-The State Horse (Winter 2007)	$6.95

UPCOMING TITLES

Tawny-The Beauty!	Black Jack-The Great!
Onie-The Roanie!	Belle-The Sweetie!
Classy-The Special!	Lily-The Pretty Paint!
Slick-The Friend!	Apple-The Joy!

Also read about Cider, Buck, Nellie, Junie, Eagle, Smokey, Sarge, Tex, Radar and many more!

ZC HORSES SERIES, 8 Hokanson Ln, Salmon, ID 83467
(208) 756-3757
www.zchorses.com Email: zchorses@hotmail.com

Please send me the books I have checked above. I am enclosing US $____(please add $2/bk or $4/order, whichever is less, to cover shipping and handling).

NAME________________________________

ADDRESS______________________________

CITY/STATE/ZIP_________________________

PHONE_______________________________

E-MAIL_______________________________

Please allow four to six weeks for delivery. Shipping prices good in U.S. only. Prices subject to change.